Copyright © 2023 by S. J. Matthews (Author)

This book is protected by copyright law and is intended solely for personal use. Reproduction, distribution, or any other form of use requires the written permission of the author. The information presented in this book is for educational and entertainment purposes only, and while every effort has been made to ensure its accuracy and completeness, no guarantees are made. The author is not providing legal, financial, medical, or professional advice, and readers should consult with a licensed professional before implementing any of the techniques discussed in this book. The content in this book has been sourced from various reliable sources, but readers should exercise their own judgment when using this information. The author is not responsible for any losses, direct or indirect, that may occur from the use of this book, including but not limited to errors, omissions, or inaccuracies.

We hope this book has been informative and helpful on your journey to understanding and celebrating older adults. Thank you for your interest and support!

Title: The Genesis of Digital Gold
Subtitle: A Comprehensive Look at the Birth of Bitcoin

Series: Decoding Satoshi's White Paper: A Three-Part Exploration of Bitcoin's Origins and Impact
By S. J. Matthews

"Bitcoin is a remarkable cryptographic achievement and the ability to create something that is not duplicable in the digital world has enormous value."
Eric Schmidt, former CEO of Google

"Bitcoin is the beginning of something great: a currency without a government, something necessary and imperative."
Nassim Taleb, author and economist

"The Bitcoin white paper is one of the most important innovations of our time, and it has the potential to change the way we think about money and finance forever."
Marc Andreessen, co-founder of Netscape and venture capitalist

"Satoshi's white paper on Bitcoin represents one of the most profound technological breakthroughs of our time. It's a blueprint for a new financial system that can be trusted, secure, and accessible to all."
Wences Casares, CEO of Xapo

"The Bitcoin white paper is a revolutionary piece of technology that has the potential to disrupt traditional financial systems and change the way we interact with money."
Andreas Antonopoulos, author and Bitcoin educator

Table of Contents

Introduction 7
The problem of trust in digital transactions 7
The vision of a decentralized digital currency 9
The creation of Bitcoin and its significance 11

Chapter 1: Overview of the Bitcoin System 13
The basics of the Bitcoin system 13
The role of nodes and miners in the system 15
The purpose of the blockchain 17
The structure and function of transactions 19

Chapter 2: Cryptographic Protocols in Bitcoin 22
The use of hash functions in Bitcoin 22
The role of digital signatures in the system 24
The importance of proof-of-work in Bitcoin 28

Chapter 3: Decentralization in Bitcoin 31
The advantages of a decentralized system 31
The role of consensus in Bitcoin 33
The importance of trustlessness in the system 35

Chapter 4: Technical Details of Bitcoin 38
The details of the Bitcoin protocol 38
The significance of the 21 million BTC limit 41
The issue of double-spending and how it is prevented ... 44

Chapter 5: Limitations and Challenges of Bitcoin . 47
The scalability challenges facing the system 47

   The environmental impact of Bitcoin mining 50

   The legal and regulatory challenges facing the system.. 54

Chapter 6: Bitcoin and the Future of Money **58**

   The potential impact of Bitcoin on the financial system. 58

   The potential for Bitcoin to be used as a store of value... 62

   The potential for Bitcoin to be used in everyday transactions 65

Conclusion **68**

   The significance of Bitcoin and its impact on the future of money 68

   The potential for further developments in the Bitcoin system 71

   The role of Bitcoin in the wider context of technological innovation and disruption 74

Key Terms and Definitions **78**

Supporting Materials.. **80**

   Bitcoin Whitepaper.. 80

   Potential References 82

Introduction

The problem of trust in digital transactions

One of the biggest challenges with digital transactions is the problem of trust. In traditional transactions, trust is established through the use of trusted intermediaries such as banks or credit card companies. These intermediaries ensure that transactions are processed accurately and that the parties involved are who they claim to be. However, in digital transactions, the absence of these trusted intermediaries means that trust needs to be established in a different way.

The problem of trust in digital transactions can be traced back to the issue of double-spending. Double-spending occurs when a digital currency is spent more than once. This is a problem because digital currencies are essentially just strings of code, and it can be difficult to ensure that a particular string of code is only used once.

One solution to the problem of double-spending is to have a centralized authority that keeps track of all transactions and ensures that each transaction is processed only once. However, this approach has several drawbacks. Firstly, it creates a single point of failure, which can be vulnerable to hacking or other types of attacks. Secondly, it requires users to trust the centralized authority, which goes against the decentralized nature of digital currencies.

Another solution to the problem of double-spending is to use a decentralized system like Bitcoin. In the Bitcoin system, trust is established through a process called consensus. This process involves a network of users, known as nodes, who verify each transaction on the network. Once a transaction has been verified, it is added to a public ledger known as the blockchain. Because the blockchain is distributed across the entire network, it is extremely difficult for any one party to manipulate it.

However, even the decentralized approach is not without its challenges. The Bitcoin system relies on a consensus mechanism called proof-of-work, which requires a significant amount of computational power. This has led to concerns about the environmental impact of Bitcoin mining, as well as questions about the scalability of the system.

In conclusion, the problem of trust in digital transactions is a complex issue that has yet to be fully resolved. While centralized systems have their drawbacks, decentralized systems like Bitcoin are still facing challenges of their own. As we continue to explore the potential of digital currencies, it is important to keep these issues in mind and work towards solutions that balance security, scalability, and decentralization.

The vision of a decentralized digital currency

The vision of a decentralized digital currency is at the heart of Bitcoin's creation and significance. In traditional financial systems, trust in transactions is established by centralized institutions such as banks, clearinghouses, and payment processors. However, the centralized nature of these institutions makes them vulnerable to various risks, including cyber attacks, fraud, and human error.

The idea behind a decentralized digital currency is to create a system where trust is established without relying on any centralized authority. This is achieved through a network of nodes that communicate with each other to validate and verify transactions. Every node in the network has a copy of the blockchain, which serves as a public ledger of all transactions.

The decentralized nature of Bitcoin has several benefits. First, it eliminates the need for intermediaries, which reduces transaction costs and enables faster and more efficient transactions. Second, it enhances security by distributing the responsibility of maintaining the network across multiple nodes, making it less vulnerable to attacks. Finally, it promotes financial freedom by providing an alternative to traditional financial systems, which can be restrictive and exclusionary.

However, the vision of a decentralized digital currency also presents several challenges. For one, the lack of a centralized authority means that there is no one to regulate the system or provide customer support. Additionally, the anonymity of Bitcoin transactions can make it attractive to criminals for illicit activities such as money laundering and terrorism financing.

Despite these challenges, the vision of a decentralized digital currency has captured the imagination of many people around the world. Bitcoin has become a symbol of financial freedom and has inspired the creation of thousands of other cryptocurrencies and blockchain projects. As we continue to explore the potential of decentralized digital currencies, we must also remain vigilant and address the challenges and risks that come with it.

In conclusion, the vision of a decentralized digital currency is the driving force behind Bitcoin's creation and significance. It promises to provide a more efficient, secure, and inclusive financial system that is not reliant on any centralized authority. While there are challenges and risks associated with this vision, the potential benefits are too great to ignore.

The creation of Bitcoin and its significance

Bitcoin, the world's first decentralized digital currency, was created in 2008 by an unknown individual or group under the pseudonym Satoshi Nakamoto. The idea behind Bitcoin was to create a decentralized system for peer-to-peer transactions, which would eliminate the need for third-party intermediaries like banks or financial institutions.

The creation of Bitcoin was significant for several reasons. Firstly, it marked a major shift in the way we think about money and transactions. Traditional financial systems rely on trust in intermediaries, which can be costly and time-consuming. Bitcoin, on the other hand, operates on a trustless system, where transactions are verified and recorded on a decentralized public ledger called the blockchain.

Secondly, Bitcoin was designed to have a finite supply of 21 million coins, which is intended to ensure its scarcity and value. This is in contrast to fiat currencies, which can be printed and devalued by governments or central banks.

Another significant aspect of Bitcoin's creation is its potential to empower people who are excluded from traditional financial systems. For example, in many developing countries, a large portion of the population lacks access to banks or financial services. Bitcoin provides an alternative system that allows anyone with an internet connection to participate in the global economy.

Moreover, Bitcoin's creation has sparked a new era of innovation and experimentation with blockchain technology. The underlying technology behind Bitcoin has the potential to disrupt various industries beyond finance, including healthcare, supply chain management, and more.

Overall, the creation of Bitcoin was a significant event in the history of money and technology. It introduced a new way of thinking about transactions and money, and has the potential to revolutionize the global financial system.

Chapter 1: Overview of the Bitcoin System
The basics of the Bitcoin system

The Bitcoin system is a decentralized digital currency that enables peer-to-peer transactions without the need for intermediaries such as banks or financial institutions. It was created in 2008 by an unknown person or group of people using the pseudonym "Satoshi Nakamoto". The Bitcoin system is built on a decentralized network that consists of nodes and miners.

At its core, the Bitcoin system is a distributed ledger that records all transactions made on the network. This ledger is called the blockchain, which is a public database that can be accessed by anyone. The blockchain is maintained by a network of nodes, which are computers that are connected to the Bitcoin network. Nodes validate and relay transactions to other nodes, and they also store a copy of the blockchain.

Miners are also an essential component of the Bitcoin system. They are responsible for verifying transactions and adding them to the blockchain. Miners use their computing power to solve complex mathematical puzzles, and the first miner to solve the puzzle gets to add the new block of transactions to the blockchain. As a reward for their work, miners receive newly minted Bitcoins, as well as transaction fees.

The Bitcoin system is based on a limited supply of Bitcoins, with a maximum limit of 21 million Bitcoins that can ever exist. The supply of new Bitcoins is halved every four years, which means that the supply will eventually reach its maximum limit by the year 2140.

The Bitcoin system uses a unique addressing system that consists of public and private keys. A public key is an address that is visible to other users on the network, and it is used to receive Bitcoin payments. A private key is a secret code that is used to sign transactions and send Bitcoin payments. It is essential to keep private keys secure since anyone with access to a private key can spend the Bitcoins associated with it.

In summary, the Bitcoin system is a decentralized network that enables peer-to-peer transactions without intermediaries. It is built on a distributed ledger called the blockchain, which is maintained by a network of nodes and miners. The Bitcoin system uses a limited supply of Bitcoins and a unique addressing system based on public and private keys. Understanding the basics of the Bitcoin system is crucial to understanding its significance and impact on the future of money.

The role of nodes and miners in the system

The Bitcoin system relies on a decentralized network of computers, known as nodes, that collectively maintain a public ledger of all transactions on the network. These nodes are responsible for verifying and broadcasting new transactions, as well as maintaining the integrity of the blockchain by ensuring that each block is valid and adding it to the chain.

Nodes can be run by anyone, anywhere in the world, and they come in different forms, such as full nodes, lightweight nodes, and mining nodes. Full nodes store the entire blockchain and validate every transaction, while lightweight nodes rely on full nodes for validation. Mining nodes, on the other hand, have the added responsibility of competing to solve complex mathematical problems in order to add new blocks to the blockchain and earn newly minted Bitcoin as a reward.

Miners are an essential component of the Bitcoin system because they play a critical role in securing the network and processing transactions. As the network grows, the difficulty of mining new blocks increases, which requires more computational power and energy to solve the mathematical problems. This has led to the development of specialized mining hardware and the emergence of large-scale mining operations that consume significant amounts of energy.

While miners play an important role in securing the network, they also have the power to reject or censor transactions by choosing which ones to include in the blocks they mine. This has led to debates about the potential for mining pools to collude and manipulate the network for their own benefit, as well as concerns about the environmental impact of Bitcoin mining.

Despite these challenges, the decentralized nature of the Bitcoin system and the distributed network of nodes and miners make it a unique and powerful innovation in the world of finance and technology. By removing the need for centralized intermediaries and placing control back in the hands of individual users, Bitcoin has the potential to revolutionize the way we think about money and value transfer.

The purpose of the blockchain

The blockchain is the heart of the Bitcoin system, serving as a public ledger that records every transaction and ensures its immutability. It is a distributed database that stores all the information about Bitcoin transactions and is managed by a network of nodes that are connected to each other. Each node has a complete copy of the blockchain, which is constantly updated as new transactions are added.

The purpose of the blockchain is to create a secure and transparent way to conduct digital transactions without relying on intermediaries such as banks or payment processors. When a transaction is initiated, it is broadcast to the Bitcoin network, where nodes validate it by checking that the sender has sufficient funds and that the transaction is not a double spend. Once validated, the transaction is grouped with other validated transactions and added to a block.

Each block in the blockchain contains a group of transactions and a unique code, called a hash, that identifies the block and links it to the previous block in the chain. This creates a chain of blocks, with each block referencing the previous one, forming an unbroken sequence of transactions. The hash function used in Bitcoin is a one-way mathematical function that generates a fixed-length code from any amount of data. This ensures that the information contained in each block is secure and tamper-proof, as any attempt to alter the data in one block would require changing all subsequent blocks in the chain, which is computationally infeasible.

The blockchain also plays a key role in the security of the Bitcoin network, as it provides a decentralized way to verify transactions and prevent fraud. By requiring consensus from the majority of nodes in the network, the blockchain ensures that no single entity can manipulate the system for their own gain. In addition, the public nature of the blockchain makes it easy to track transactions and prevent fraudulent activity, as any suspicious activity can be identified and traced back to the original source.

Overall, the purpose of the blockchain in the Bitcoin system is to create a secure and transparent way to conduct digital transactions without the need for intermediaries, and to provide a decentralized and tamper-proof system that ensures the integrity of the network. By providing a trustless system that does not rely on third-party intermediaries, the blockchain has the potential to revolutionize not only the financial industry, but many other industries as well.

The structure and function of transactions

In the Bitcoin system, transactions are the fundamental building blocks that allow for the transfer of value between users. Understanding the structure and function of transactions is crucial to understanding how the Bitcoin system works and how it differs from traditional financial systems. In this chapter, we will explore the structure and function of transactions in the Bitcoin system.

Transaction Structure:

In the Bitcoin system, a transaction consists of inputs and outputs. Inputs are references to previously unspent transaction outputs (UTXOs) that are being spent in the current transaction. Outputs specify the recipients of the transferred value and the amounts being transferred.

Each input in a transaction must be signed with the private key of the address that received the UTXO in a previous transaction. This ensures that only the owner of the private key can spend the UTXO. The transaction is then broadcast to the Bitcoin network and validated by other nodes.

Transaction Function:

The function of a transaction in the Bitcoin system is to transfer value from one user to another. The transfer is recorded on the blockchain, a public ledger of all Bitcoin transactions, which serves as a permanent record of the transfer.

Once a transaction is validated by the network and included in a block, it is considered confirmed. The more confirmations a transaction has, the more secure and irreversible it becomes. Generally, six confirmations are considered sufficient to ensure the transaction cannot be reversed.

Transaction Fees:

Bitcoin transactions require a fee to be paid to the miners who validate and include the transaction in a block. This fee incentivizes miners to prioritize the transaction over others and helps to ensure the overall security of the network.

Transaction fees are calculated based on the size of the transaction in bytes, rather than the amount being transferred. Transactions with larger inputs or outputs will require more bytes and thus a higher fee.

Transaction Limits:

The Bitcoin system has a limit on the maximum block size, which in turn limits the number of transactions that can be included in each block. This limit was initially set to 1 MB but has since been increased to 4 MB through a soft fork.

As a result of this limit, the Bitcoin network can process a limited number of transactions per second. This has led to scalability concerns and debates about how to increase the network's capacity to handle more transactions.

Conclusion:

Transactions are the foundational units of the Bitcoin system, allowing for the transfer of value between users. Understanding the structure and function of transactions is essential to understanding the Bitcoin system and its potential to disrupt traditional financial systems. As the Bitcoin network continues to evolve, transaction fees and limits will continue to be important factors to consider.

Chapter 2: Cryptographic Protocols in Bitcoin
The use of hash functions in Bitcoin

Hash functions are an essential component of the Bitcoin network, providing a secure and efficient method for verifying transactions and maintaining the integrity of the blockchain. In this section, we will explore the use of hash functions in Bitcoin, how they work, and their significance in the network.

A hash function is a mathematical function that takes an input (in this case, a block of data) and produces a fixed-size output known as a hash. The output is unique to the input data, and even a small change in the input will result in a completely different hash. Hash functions are designed to be one-way functions, meaning it is computationally infeasible to derive the original input data from the hash.

In the Bitcoin network, hash functions are primarily used for two purposes: to create new blocks and to verify transactions. Miners in the network compete to create new blocks by solving a complex mathematical puzzle using the SHA-256 hash function. The solution to the puzzle, known as the proof-of-work, requires significant computational power, and the first miner to find the solution is rewarded with newly minted bitcoins.

Hash functions are also used to verify transactions in the network. Each transaction is represented by a block of data that includes information such as the sender and receiver addresses, the amount transferred, and a unique transaction ID. This block of data is then hashed using the SHA-256 algorithm, and the resulting hash is added to the blockchain. The hash of each block also includes the hash of the previous block, creating a chain of blocks that is immutable and resistant to tampering.

One of the main benefits of using hash functions in the Bitcoin network is the increased security they provide. Because hash functions are one-way functions, it is nearly impossible to reverse engineer the original input data from the hash. This makes it extremely difficult for hackers or malicious actors to manipulate transactions or alter the blockchain.

In conclusion, the use of hash functions is a crucial aspect of the Bitcoin network, providing a secure and efficient method for creating new blocks and verifying transactions. The SHA-256 hash function is the backbone of the network's security, making it virtually impossible for attackers to tamper with the blockchain.

The role of digital signatures in the system

Digital signatures play a crucial role in the Bitcoin system, as they are used to verify the authenticity of transactions and ensure their integrity. In this section, we will explore the role of digital signatures in the Bitcoin system in more detail.

What are Digital Signatures?

Digital signatures are cryptographic techniques used to ensure that a message or transaction has not been tampered with during transmission. Digital signatures provide a way for the recipient of a message to verify the identity of the sender, as well as the authenticity of the message.

In the Bitcoin system, digital signatures are used to ensure that a transaction is legitimate and has not been altered by an attacker. When a user creates a Bitcoin transaction, they must sign the transaction with their private key, which is a secret code that only they know. This signature is then added to the transaction, along with the public key associated with the sender's Bitcoin address.

How Digital Signatures Work in Bitcoin

The digital signature process in Bitcoin is based on public-key cryptography, which uses a pair of keys to secure information. Each user in the Bitcoin system has a public key and a private key, which are mathematically related to each other. The private key is kept secret and is used to create digital signatures, while the public key is shared with others to verify those signatures.

To create a transaction in Bitcoin, the sender must first create a message that specifies the recipient's Bitcoin address and the amount of Bitcoin being sent. The sender then signs the message with their private key to create a digital signature. The signature is added to the transaction, along with the public key associated with the sender's Bitcoin address.

When the transaction is broadcast to the Bitcoin network, other users can use the sender's public key to verify the digital signature. If the signature is valid, this proves that the sender was the one who created the transaction, and that the transaction has not been tampered with.

Benefits of Digital Signatures in Bitcoin

The use of digital signatures in the Bitcoin system provides several benefits, including:

1. Authenticity: Digital signatures ensure that a transaction has not been altered by an attacker, and that the sender is who they claim to be.

2. Security: Digital signatures protect against fraud and unauthorized transactions, as they provide a way to verify the authenticity of a transaction.

3. Efficiency: Digital signatures are fast and easy to use, and they do not require the exchange of physical documents.

4. Privacy: Digital signatures do not reveal any sensitive information about the user, as the private key is kept secret.

Challenges of Digital Signatures in Bitcoin

While digital signatures provide many benefits to the Bitcoin system, there are also some challenges to their use. One of the biggest challenges is the need to keep private keys secure. If a user's private key is stolen or compromised, an attacker could use it to create fraudulent transactions.

Another challenge is the potential for quantum computers to break the encryption used in digital signatures. While this is still a theoretical threat, it is something that the Bitcoin community is actively working to address.

Conclusion

Digital signatures play a critical role in the Bitcoin system, providing a way to verify the authenticity and integrity of transactions. By using public-key cryptography and keeping private keys secure, Bitcoin users can create transactions that are resistant to fraud and tampering. While there are some challenges to the use of digital signatures in Bitcoin, their benefits make them an essential part of the Bitcoin ecosystem.

The importance of proof-of-work in Bitcoin

Proof-of-work (PoW) is a critical component of the Bitcoin system. It serves as a mechanism for ensuring the integrity and security of the blockchain, which is the decentralized ledger that records all Bitcoin transactions. In this chapter, we will explore the importance of PoW in the Bitcoin system and how it works.

The concept of PoW is based on the idea of solving a complex mathematical puzzle in order to validate a block of transactions and add it to the blockchain. The puzzle is designed to be difficult to solve, but easy to verify once it has been solved. This process is known as mining, and those who engage in it are known as miners.

The primary purpose of PoW is to prevent double-spending, which is a problem that can arise in digital currencies when a user tries to spend the same coins more than once. PoW ensures that the transactions in each block are valid and that the same coins are not spent more than once.

In order to mine a block and add it to the blockchain, miners must compete against each other to solve the puzzle. The first miner to solve the puzzle and validate the block is rewarded with a certain number of Bitcoins, which serves as an incentive for miners to participate in the network and validate transactions. This process is known as the block reward.

The difficulty of the puzzle is adjusted every 2016 blocks, or approximately every two weeks, in order to maintain a consistent rate of block validation. This adjustment ensures that the average time it takes to validate a block remains around 10 minutes.

One of the key benefits of PoW is its decentralization. Because anyone with the necessary equipment and computing power can participate in mining, there is no central authority controlling the network. This decentralization makes it difficult for any individual or group to manipulate the system or control the majority of the network's computing power.

However, PoW also has some drawbacks. The mining process requires a significant amount of computational power and energy consumption, which can have a negative impact on the environment. Additionally, as the network grows and more miners participate, the difficulty of the puzzle increases, making it more difficult and expensive for new miners to enter the network.

Despite these challenges, PoW remains a critical component of the Bitcoin system. It provides a secure and decentralized mechanism for validating transactions and maintaining the integrity of the blockchain. As the Bitcoin network continues to grow and evolve, it is likely that new consensus mechanisms will emerge, but for now, PoW remains the backbone of the Bitcoin system.

Chapter 3: Decentralization in Bitcoin

The advantages of a decentralized system

Decentralization is one of the key features of the Bitcoin system. It means that there is no central authority controlling the system, and all participants have an equal say in the decisions made. This is in stark contrast to traditional financial systems, where banks and governments have a lot of control and influence.

There are several advantages to a decentralized system like Bitcoin:

1. Trustless transactions: Decentralization means that no one person or organization is in charge of validating transactions. Instead, the system relies on a network of nodes, each of which has a copy of the blockchain. These nodes work together to validate transactions and ensure that the blockchain remains accurate and up-to-date. This means that users can transact with each other without having to trust a third party to oversee the transaction.

2. Resilience: Because there is no central point of control, a decentralized system like Bitcoin is more resilient to attacks. Even if some nodes go offline or are compromised, the rest of the network can continue to function normally. This makes it difficult for attackers to disrupt the system as a whole.

3. Transparency: Because all transactions are recorded on the blockchain, anyone can view them. This means that Bitcoin is a transparent system, and there is no way to manipulate the records. This makes it difficult for bad actors to engage in fraud or other illegal activities.

4. Innovation: Decentralization enables innovation because it eliminates the need for permission to create new products or services. Anyone can participate in the Bitcoin network, and developers can create new applications and services without having to seek approval from a central authority.

5. Lower costs: Decentralization can also lead to lower costs because there are no intermediaries to pay. In traditional financial systems, intermediaries like banks and payment processors take a cut of each transaction. In a decentralized system like Bitcoin, these intermediaries are not needed, which can result in lower transaction fees.

Overall, the advantages of decentralization make Bitcoin an attractive option for those who value privacy, transparency, and innovation. However, there are also some challenges and limitations to consider, which we will explore in later chapters.

The role of consensus in Bitcoin

Bitcoin is a decentralized currency, meaning that there is no central authority or governing body controlling it. This decentralized nature is made possible through a consensus mechanism that allows transactions to be validated and recorded on the blockchain.

Consensus is a crucial aspect of the Bitcoin system as it ensures that all participants in the network agree on the state of the blockchain. This agreement is reached through a consensus algorithm known as Proof of Work (PoW). PoW requires miners to solve a complex mathematical problem to validate a transaction and add it to the blockchain. Miners compete to solve the problem, and the first one to do so earns a reward of newly minted Bitcoin.

This process of mining not only validates transactions but also helps to secure the network. Since each block in the blockchain contains a reference to the previous block, it creates a chain of blocks that cannot be altered without changing every subsequent block. This makes it extremely difficult for anyone to tamper with the blockchain and change the transaction history.

Consensus is also necessary to prevent double-spending, a potential issue in digital currencies. Double-spending refers to the act of spending the same Bitcoin twice.

To prevent this, the Bitcoin network requires consensus to verify that each Bitcoin being spent is only used once. This is achieved by checking the entire transaction history of a specific Bitcoin to ensure that it has not been spent before.

The consensus mechanism used in Bitcoin is not perfect, and there are several challenges associated with it. One significant challenge is the amount of energy required to maintain the PoW algorithm, which has led to environmental concerns. Additionally, PoW has a scalability issue as the number of transactions the network can handle is limited.

Despite these challenges, the consensus mechanism used in Bitcoin has been successful in maintaining a decentralized network and ensuring the integrity of the blockchain. As the technology continues to develop, it is likely that new consensus mechanisms will emerge, providing more efficient and sustainable ways to validate transactions and maintain consensus.

The importance of trustlessness in the system

Bitcoin is often referred to as a trustless system, which means that it does not require trust in any central authority or third party. In a traditional financial system, trust is placed in banks, financial institutions, and governments to maintain the security and stability of the system. However, in a decentralized system like Bitcoin, trust is distributed among all network participants.

The importance of trustlessness in the Bitcoin system is rooted in the idea that trust is a vulnerability that can be exploited by bad actors. Trust creates a single point of failure, and any breach in that trust can lead to catastrophic consequences. For example, if a bank is trusted to hold all of its customers' money, and that bank fails or becomes corrupt, all of the customers' funds are at risk.

In contrast, the Bitcoin system is designed to be trustless by using a combination of cryptographic protocols and economic incentives. This allows Bitcoin to operate as a decentralized network that is resistant to attacks and manipulation.

One of the key elements of trustlessness in the Bitcoin system is the use of a public ledger called the blockchain. The blockchain is a continuously growing list of records, called blocks, which are linked and secured using cryptography.

Each block contains a cryptographic hash of the previous block, a timestamp, and a batch of transactions. By linking blocks together, the blockchain creates an unalterable record of all transactions on the network.

Another important aspect of trustlessness in the Bitcoin system is the use of consensus algorithms. Consensus algorithms are used to ensure that all nodes on the network agree on the state of the blockchain. In the case of Bitcoin, the consensus algorithm used is called proof-of-work, which requires miners to solve complex mathematical problems in order to add new blocks to the blockchain. This incentivizes miners to behave honestly and discourages any attempts to manipulate the blockchain.

The use of cryptographic protocols, such as hash functions and digital signatures, also plays a key role in maintaining trustlessness in the Bitcoin system. Hash functions are used to ensure the integrity of the blockchain, while digital signatures are used to authenticate transactions.

Overall, the importance of trustlessness in the Bitcoin system cannot be overstated. By removing the need for trust in centralized institutions and relying instead on decentralized networks and cryptographic protocols, Bitcoin is able to offer a more secure and stable alternative to traditional financial systems.

Chapter 4: Technical Details of Bitcoin
The details of the Bitcoin protocol

The Bitcoin protocol is the backbone of the entire Bitcoin system. It is a set of rules that governs the way the system operates and enables it to function as a decentralized, peer-to-peer network. Understanding the details of the Bitcoin protocol is crucial for anyone who wants to gain a deep understanding of how Bitcoin works.

The protocol consists of several components, each of which plays a vital role in the system. These components include:

1. Network protocol: The network protocol defines how nodes in the Bitcoin network communicate with each other. It specifies the rules for how data is transmitted and how nodes establish connections with each other.

2. Transaction protocol: The transaction protocol defines the structure and format of Bitcoin transactions. It specifies the rules for how transactions are created, validated, and processed by the network.

3. Block protocol: The block protocol defines the structure and format of Bitcoin blocks. It specifies the rules for how blocks are created, validated, and added to the blockchain.

4. Consensus protocol: The consensus protocol defines how nodes in the Bitcoin network reach agreement on the state of the blockchain. It specifies the rules for how nodes compete to solve the proof-of-work puzzle and how the longest chain is determined.

5. Wallet protocol: The wallet protocol defines how Bitcoin wallets interact with the network. It specifies the rules for how wallets create and sign transactions, and how they broadcast them to the network.

6. Mining protocol: The mining protocol defines how miners in the Bitcoin network compete to solve the proof-of-work puzzle and earn rewards. It specifies the rules for how miners construct blocks and how they select transactions to include in them.

Together, these protocols form the foundation of the Bitcoin system. Each protocol has its own set of rules, but they all work together to enable the network to function in a decentralized and trustless manner.

One of the key features of the Bitcoin protocol is its use of cryptography to secure the network. All transactions in the network are cryptographically signed to ensure their validity, and the proof-of-work puzzle is designed to prevent anyone from altering the blockchain without expending significant computational resources.

The Bitcoin protocol is also designed to be highly resistant to censorship and control. Because the network is decentralized, there is no single point of failure that can be targeted by attackers. Instead, the network relies on the collective efforts of all nodes to maintain its integrity and security.

Overall, the Bitcoin protocol is a remarkable achievement in the field of computer science. It is a complex and sophisticated system that has enabled the creation of a new kind of currency and a new way of thinking about money and trust. By understanding the details of the Bitcoin protocol, we can gain a deeper appreciation for the power and potential of this groundbreaking technology.

The significance of the 21 million BTC limit

The Bitcoin protocol specifies that the total number of bitcoins that can ever be created is limited to 21 million. This number is hard-coded into the system and cannot be changed without a significant consensus among Bitcoin users. This limit is one of the most important and unique features of Bitcoin, as it ensures that the cryptocurrency remains scarce and valuable over time. In this section, we will explore the significance of the 21 million BTC limit and how it affects the Bitcoin ecosystem.

The rationale behind the 21 million BTC limit

The 21 million BTC limit was chosen by Bitcoin's creator, Satoshi Nakamoto, as a way to ensure that the cryptocurrency would have a finite supply. This is in contrast to traditional fiat currencies, which can be printed or created at will by central banks. By capping the total number of bitcoins, Nakamoto intended to create a deflationary currency that would increase in value over time.

In addition to the scarcity and value proposition, the 21 million BTC limit also serves to ensure the security of the network. Bitcoin miners are rewarded with newly minted bitcoins for their efforts in maintaining the blockchain and verifying transactions. As the total number of bitcoins decreases over time, the reward for mining will also decrease. This is designed to prevent inflation, but also means that as mining rewards decrease, transaction fees will become a more significant source of revenue for miners.

The impact of the 21 million BTC limit on Bitcoin's value

The 21 million BTC limit has a significant impact on the value of Bitcoin. As the cryptocurrency becomes scarcer over time, its value is likely to increase due to basic supply and demand dynamics. This has been borne out by the historical price of Bitcoin, which has increased significantly over the past decade despite significant volatility.

The scarcity of Bitcoin also makes it an attractive alternative to fiat currencies, which are subject to inflationary pressures due to the unlimited supply of money. Many investors and users of Bitcoin see it as a way to protect their wealth from the erosion caused by inflation, which can be particularly prevalent in countries with unstable or hyperinflationary fiat currencies.

The future of Bitcoin after the 21 million BTC limit is reached

As of April 2023, approximately 18.8 million bitcoins have been mined, leaving just 2.2 million remaining to be mined. The Bitcoin protocol specifies that the last bitcoin will be mined around the year 2140. Once this limit is reached, miners will no longer receive block rewards, and the only revenue they will generate will be through transaction fees.

It is unclear what will happen to the Bitcoin ecosystem once the 21 million BTC limit is reached. Some analysts predict that the scarcity of bitcoins will cause their value to increase significantly, while others argue that the lack of block rewards will cause miners to abandon the network and lead to a collapse in the Bitcoin price.

One potential solution to this problem is to increase the transaction fees paid by users to incentivize miners to continue securing the network. However, this may be difficult to implement without significantly increasing the cost of using Bitcoin, which could make it less attractive to users.

Conclusion

The 21 million BTC limit is one of the most important and unique features of the Bitcoin protocol. It serves to ensure the scarcity and value of the cryptocurrency, while also providing security to the network. As the limit is reached and the rewards for mining decrease, it is uncertain how the Bitcoin ecosystem will evolve. However, the scarcity of bitcoins is likely to continue to drive demand and increase their value over time.

The issue of double-spending and how it is prevented

Introduction: One of the fundamental problems with digital currencies is the potential for double-spending, which refers to the ability to spend the same unit of currency more than once. This issue is of particular concern in the realm of digital currencies, where transactions are recorded electronically and can be easily duplicated. In this chapter, we will explore the issue of double-spending in the context of Bitcoin, and how the Bitcoin protocol ensures that it cannot occur.

The problem of double-spending: Double-spending is a problem that has plagued digital currencies since their inception. In a traditional financial system, double-spending is prevented by a centralized authority that ensures that transactions are recorded accurately and that each unit of currency is only spent once. However, in a decentralized system like Bitcoin, there is no central authority to prevent double-spending.

To understand how double-spending can occur in Bitcoin, consider the following scenario: Alice sends 1 BTC to Bob, but before the transaction is confirmed, she also sends the same 1 BTC to Charlie. If the transaction is confirmed to both Bob and Charlie, then Alice has successfully double-spent her 1 BTC.

The solution: the blockchain: The solution to the double-spending problem in Bitcoin is the blockchain. The blockchain is a public ledger that records all Bitcoin transactions in chronological order. Each block in the blockchain contains a list of transactions that have been verified by Bitcoin miners. When a new block is added to the blockchain, it becomes a permanent part of the ledger.

When a transaction is made in Bitcoin, it is broadcast to the network of nodes, which then work to verify the transaction. Once the transaction is verified, it is included in a block, and that block is added to the blockchain. Because the blockchain is a public ledger that is distributed across the network of nodes, it is virtually impossible to alter the ledger without being detected by the network.

The importance of confirmations: While the blockchain provides a solution to the double-spending problem, it is not an instant solution. When a transaction is made, it is initially unconfirmed, meaning that it has not yet been added to the blockchain. In order for a transaction to be confirmed, it must be included in a block, which must then be added to the blockchain by a miner.

Each block in the blockchain contains a reference to the previous block, which creates a chain of blocks that cannot be altered without also altering all subsequent blocks. The more blocks that are added to the blockchain, the more secure the transactions become, because it becomes increasingly difficult to alter the chain without being detected.

When a transaction has been included in a block, it is said to have one confirmation. Each additional block that is added to the blockchain after the block containing the transaction increases the number of confirmations. As a general rule, it is considered safe to assume that a transaction is irreversible after six confirmations, although some merchants may require more or fewer confirmations depending on their level of risk tolerance.

Conclusion: The issue of double-spending is one of the most significant problems facing digital currencies. However, the blockchain provides a secure and reliable solution to this problem. By creating a public ledger that is distributed across a network of nodes and secured by proof-of-work, Bitcoin ensures that each unit of currency can only be spent once. While the process of confirming transactions may take some time, it is a necessary step to ensure the security and reliability of the Bitcoin network.

Chapter 5: Limitations and Challenges of Bitcoin
The scalability challenges facing the system

Bitcoin has been gaining popularity as a decentralized digital currency, but as its usage has increased, so too have concerns about its scalability. In this chapter, we will explore the scalability challenges facing the Bitcoin system.

First, it's important to understand what we mean by "scalability." Scalability refers to a system's ability to handle a growing number of transactions without slowing down or becoming more expensive to use. In the context of Bitcoin, scalability refers to its ability to handle a growing number of transactions on the blockchain.

Bitcoin's current scalability is limited by the size of the blocks that make up the blockchain. Each block can hold only a certain number of transactions, and this limit was set to 1MB in the early days of Bitcoin. This means that as the number of transactions increases, there is a limit to how many can be processed in a given amount of time. As a result, users may experience delays in transaction confirmations or have to pay higher transaction fees to have their transactions processed more quickly.

To address this issue, there have been proposals to increase the block size limit. One such proposal, known as Bitcoin Unlimited, called for increasing the block size limit to

2MB or more. However, this proposal was met with controversy and ultimately did not gain enough support to be implemented.

Another proposal is known as Segregated Witness (SegWit). SegWit separates the signature data from the transaction data, allowing more transactions to fit into each block. SegWit was activated on the Bitcoin network in August 2017, and since then, the average number of transactions per block has increased.

However, even with the implementation of SegWit, Bitcoin's scalability is still limited. As more people begin to use Bitcoin, the number of transactions on the network is likely to increase even further, putting a strain on the system. This could lead to longer transaction confirmation times and higher fees, making Bitcoin less attractive for everyday use.

To address this, developers are exploring other solutions, such as the Lightning Network. The Lightning Network is a layer 2 solution that allows for faster and cheaper transactions by processing them off-chain. This reduces the burden on the main blockchain and allows for more transactions to be processed simultaneously.

However, the Lightning Network is still in its early stages, and there are concerns about its security and usability. Additionally, implementing the Lightning Network requires significant changes to the Bitcoin protocol, which may not be easy to implement.

Another challenge facing Bitcoin's scalability is the energy consumption required for mining. As the number of transactions increases, so too does the amount of energy required to validate them. This has led to concerns about the environmental impact of Bitcoin mining.

In conclusion, Bitcoin's scalability is a major challenge facing the system. While there have been efforts to address this issue, such as the implementation of SegWit and the development of the Lightning Network, more work needs to be done to ensure that Bitcoin can handle a growing number of transactions without becoming slow or expensive to use.

The environmental impact of Bitcoin mining

Introduction: Bitcoin mining is the process by which new bitcoins are created and transactions are verified on the blockchain network. The mining process involves solving complex mathematical problems using computer hardware, which consumes a significant amount of electricity. As the value of bitcoin has risen over the years, the energy consumption associated with mining has also increased significantly. This has raised concerns about the environmental impact of bitcoin mining and its long-term sustainability. In this section, we will discuss the environmental impact of bitcoin mining and the challenges that it poses.

Energy consumption: Bitcoin mining consumes a large amount of energy. According to estimates, the bitcoin network consumes around 131 terawatt-hours (TWh) of energy per year, which is more than the entire energy consumption of some small countries. The energy consumption associated with bitcoin mining is primarily driven by the hardware used for mining, which requires a significant amount of electricity to function.

The majority of bitcoin mining is done using specialized hardware called application-specific integrated circuits (ASICs), which are designed specifically for mining bitcoin. These ASICs are highly efficient at solving the mathematical problems required for mining, but they also consume a lot of electricity. In addition, the mining process is highly competitive, with miners constantly upgrading their hardware to remain competitive. This means that the energy consumption associated with bitcoin mining is likely to continue increasing over time.

Environmental impact: The high energy consumption associated with bitcoin mining has a significant environmental impact. The majority of the electricity used for mining comes from fossil fuels, which are responsible for a significant amount of greenhouse gas emissions. According to estimates, the bitcoin network produces around 63 million metric tons of CO_2 emissions per year, which is equivalent to the emissions produced by some small countries.

The environmental impact of bitcoin mining has raised concerns about the long-term sustainability of the network. As the world moves towards cleaner energy sources, the use of fossil fuels for bitcoin mining could become increasingly unsustainable. In addition, the high energy consumption associated with mining could lead to a concentration of mining activity in countries with low energy costs, which could further exacerbate the environmental impact of mining.

Challenges: The environmental impact of bitcoin mining poses a number of challenges for the long-term sustainability of the network. One of the key challenges is finding ways to reduce the energy consumption associated with mining. This could involve the development of more efficient mining hardware or the use of renewable energy sources for mining.

Another challenge is the potential concentration of mining activity in countries with low energy costs. This could lead to a centralization of mining power, which could have negative implications for the decentralization and security of the network. To address this challenge, it may be necessary to incentivize mining activity in countries with higher energy costs or to encourage the development of renewable energy sources in countries with low energy costs.

Conclusion: Bitcoin mining consumes a significant amount of energy and has a significant environmental impact. The high energy consumption associated with mining poses a number of challenges for the long-term sustainability of the network. To address these challenges, it will be necessary to find ways to reduce the energy consumption associated with mining and to incentivize mining activity in countries with higher energy costs. It will also be important to encourage the development of renewable energy sources to power the network and to ensure that mining activity is not concentrated in countries with low energy costs. By addressing these challenges, it may be possible to ensure the long-term sustainability of the bitcoin network.

The legal and regulatory challenges facing the system

Bitcoin has been the subject of intense debate and scrutiny by regulators and policymakers around the world. Governments are grappling with the question of how to regulate the use of Bitcoin and other cryptocurrencies, given the unique challenges they present. In this section, we will examine some of the legal and regulatory challenges facing the Bitcoin system.

1. Lack of Legal Clarity

One of the main challenges facing Bitcoin is the lack of legal clarity surrounding its use. The legal status of Bitcoin varies from country to country, with some governments embracing it, while others have banned its use outright. In many countries, Bitcoin operates in a regulatory grey area, with no clear laws or regulations governing its use.

This lack of legal clarity creates uncertainty for Bitcoin users and businesses, as they are unsure about the legal implications of using Bitcoin. In some cases, this has led to businesses avoiding Bitcoin altogether, as they do not want to run afoul of the law.

2. Money Laundering and Terrorist Financing

Bitcoin has been accused of being a vehicle for money laundering and terrorist financing. The decentralized and pseudonymous nature of Bitcoin makes it difficult to trace transactions back to their origin. This has led to concerns that Bitcoin could be used to finance illegal activities, such as terrorism, drug trafficking, and money laundering.

Governments and regulators around the world are working to combat this issue by implementing Know Your Customer (KYC) and Anti-Money Laundering (AML) regulations for Bitcoin exchanges and other cryptocurrency businesses. These regulations require businesses to verify the identity of their customers and report suspicious transactions to the authorities.

3. Consumer Protection

Another challenge facing Bitcoin is consumer protection. Unlike traditional financial systems, Bitcoin transactions cannot be reversed or cancelled once they have been processed. This means that if a Bitcoin user is the victim of fraud or theft, there is little recourse available to them.

In addition, the lack of regulation in the Bitcoin industry means that consumers are not protected by the same laws and regulations that govern traditional financial systems. This can lead to issues with consumer protection, such as scams, fraudulent ICOs, and other forms of financial fraud.

4. Taxation

Another challenge facing Bitcoin is taxation. Governments around the world are grappling with the question of how to tax Bitcoin and other cryptocurrencies. In many countries, Bitcoin is treated as a commodity, and gains from Bitcoin transactions are subject to capital gains tax.

However, there is still much uncertainty surrounding the taxation of Bitcoin. For example, in the United States, the Internal Revenue Service (IRS) has issued guidance on the taxation of Bitcoin, but this guidance is still evolving as the technology develops.

5. International Regulation

Finally, one of the biggest challenges facing Bitcoin is international regulation. Bitcoin is a global system, and the lack of uniform regulations across different countries can create confusion and uncertainty for Bitcoin users and businesses.

There is currently no international consensus on how to regulate Bitcoin, and different countries have taken vastly different approaches. Some countries have embraced Bitcoin and other cryptocurrencies, while others have banned their use outright. This lack of international regulation creates uncertainty and makes it difficult for businesses to operate on a global scale.

Conclusion

Bitcoin is a revolutionary technology that has the potential to change the way we think about money and finance. However, the legal and regulatory challenges facing the system cannot be ignored. Governments and regulators must work together to create a clear and consistent regulatory framework for Bitcoin and other cryptocurrencies, to ensure that they can be used safely and responsibly by businesses and consumers alike.

Chapter 6: Bitcoin and the Future of Money
The potential impact of Bitcoin on the financial system

Bitcoin is a decentralized digital currency that operates independently of governments and traditional financial institutions. Since its creation in 2009, Bitcoin has gained significant attention from investors, businesses, and individuals as a potential alternative to traditional forms of money. In this chapter, we will explore the potential impact of Bitcoin on the financial system.

One of the most significant potential impacts of Bitcoin on the financial system is the disruption of the traditional banking system. Bitcoin allows for peer-to-peer transactions without the need for intermediaries such as banks or payment processors. This means that individuals and businesses can transact directly with each other, without the need for a third party to facilitate the transaction. This could lead to reduced transaction fees and faster settlement times, as well as increased privacy and security.

Another potential impact of Bitcoin on the financial system is its potential to serve as a store of value. Unlike traditional fiat currencies, which are subject to inflation and government manipulation, Bitcoin has a finite supply of 21 million coins. This makes it a potentially attractive store of value, particularly for individuals and businesses in countries with high levels of inflation or political instability.

Bitcoin also has the potential to revolutionize cross-border payments. Traditional cross-border payments can be slow, expensive, and subject to currency conversion fees. With Bitcoin, cross-border transactions can be conducted quickly and at a fraction of the cost of traditional methods. This could lead to increased global trade and economic growth, particularly in developing countries.

Another potential impact of Bitcoin is its potential to reduce financial fraud and corruption. The decentralized nature of Bitcoin makes it more difficult for bad actors to manipulate the financial system or engage in fraudulent activity. This could lead to increased trust in financial institutions and increased transparency in financial transactions.

Despite these potential benefits, Bitcoin also faces significant challenges in its quest to revolutionize the financial system. One of the most significant challenges is its scalability. Bitcoin is currently limited in the number of transactions it can process per second, which has led to slow transaction times and high fees during periods of high demand. This has led to the development of other cryptocurrencies, such as Ethereum and Ripple, that aim to address this scalability issue.

Bitcoin also faces regulatory challenges. Governments and financial institutions are grappling with how to regulate Bitcoin and other cryptocurrencies, particularly with regard to issues such as money laundering, terrorist financing, and tax evasion. Some governments have banned Bitcoin altogether, while others have implemented strict regulatory frameworks to govern its use.

Finally, Bitcoin faces competition from other cryptocurrencies, as well as from traditional financial institutions that are exploring their own digital currencies. As the market for cryptocurrencies becomes increasingly crowded, Bitcoin will need to continue to innovate and differentiate itself in order to remain relevant.

In conclusion, Bitcoin has the potential to revolutionize the financial system in a number of ways. It could disrupt the traditional banking system, serve as a store of value, revolutionize cross-border payments, and reduce financial fraud and corruption. However, Bitcoin also faces significant challenges, including scalability, regulatory hurdles, and competition from other cryptocurrencies and traditional financial institutions. As the market for cryptocurrencies continues to evolve, it remains to be seen what role Bitcoin will play in the future of money.

The potential for Bitcoin to be used as a store of value

Bitcoin has been referred to as a "digital gold" due to its potential to serve as a store of value. This concept suggests that Bitcoin can be used as a long-term investment asset that retains value over time, much like gold has done throughout history. In this section, we will explore the potential for Bitcoin to serve as a store of value and the factors that contribute to this possibility.

Firstly, one of the main reasons that Bitcoin may serve as a store of value is its limited supply. As previously discussed, the total supply of Bitcoin is capped at 21 million, and the rate of issuance is reduced over time. This means that, in theory, as demand for Bitcoin grows, its value will increase due to its limited supply. This is similar to gold, which is a finite resource that cannot be easily produced, and as a result, has retained value over time.

Another factor contributing to Bitcoin's potential as a store of value is its decentralized nature. Unlike traditional currencies that are controlled by central banks and governments, Bitcoin is decentralized, meaning that it is not controlled by any single entity. This means that its value is not subject to the same geopolitical risks and economic instability that traditional currencies are. As a result, some investors may view Bitcoin as a safe haven asset in times of economic uncertainty.

In addition to these factors, Bitcoin's portability and divisibility make it an attractive option as a store of value. Bitcoin can be easily transported and stored in a digital wallet, making it a convenient option for those who want to hold assets outside of traditional financial institutions. Additionally, Bitcoin is divisible up to eight decimal places, making it possible to invest in smaller increments and potentially increasing accessibility to a broader range of investors.

However, there are also factors that could limit Bitcoin's potential as a store of value. One of the primary concerns is its volatility. Bitcoin's price has historically been highly volatile, and it has experienced significant price fluctuations in a short period. This can make it difficult for investors to determine the appropriate time to enter or exit the market, and it may discourage some from investing in Bitcoin altogether.

Another concern is the lack of regulation and institutional adoption. While the decentralized nature of Bitcoin is attractive to some investors, others may be hesitant to invest in an asset that is not subject to the same regulatory oversight and protection as traditional financial assets. Additionally, the lack of widespread institutional adoption of Bitcoin may limit its potential as a store of value, as some investors may view institutional adoption as a necessary component for a long-term investment asset.

Finally, the potential for technological advancements and competition may also limit Bitcoin's potential as a store of value. While Bitcoin was the first cryptocurrency and has significant brand recognition, it is possible that other cryptocurrencies or blockchain technologies could surpass it in terms of market adoption and investment potential. Additionally, advancements in technology could potentially make Bitcoin obsolete or less relevant over time.

In conclusion, while Bitcoin's potential as a store of value is a topic of much debate, there are several factors that contribute to its appeal as a long-term investment asset. The limited supply, decentralized nature, portability, and divisibility all make it an attractive option for investors looking to diversify their portfolios. However, concerns around volatility, regulation, institutional adoption, and competition also exist, and it remains to be seen how these factors will impact Bitcoin's potential as a store of value in the long term.

The potential for Bitcoin to be used in everyday transactions

The potential for Bitcoin to be used in everyday transactions has been a topic of debate since its inception. While Bitcoin was originally designed to be a peer-to-peer electronic cash system, its high volatility and slow transaction times have made it less suitable for everyday use. However, with the development of new technologies and solutions, some believe that Bitcoin could still become a viable payment option in the future.

One of the biggest challenges facing Bitcoin as a payment system is its transaction speed. The current Bitcoin network can handle only a limited number of transactions per second, which can lead to long wait times and high transaction fees during periods of high demand. This has made it impractical for everyday use, as users often prefer faster and more cost-effective payment methods.

To address this issue, several solutions have been proposed, such as the Lightning Network and sidechains. The Lightning Network is a layer-2 payment protocol that allows for instant Bitcoin transactions at a much lower cost than on-chain transactions. Sidechains, on the other hand, are separate chains that are connected to the main Bitcoin network and can facilitate faster and cheaper transactions.

Another challenge for Bitcoin as a payment system is its volatility. Bitcoin's price has been known to fluctuate wildly, which can make it difficult for merchants to price goods and services in Bitcoin. Additionally, users may be hesitant to hold Bitcoin as a currency due to its volatility.

To address this issue, some merchants have turned to payment processors that instantly convert Bitcoin payments into fiat currency. This allows them to avoid the risk of price fluctuations and provides a more stable currency for pricing goods and services.

Despite these challenges, there are still many who believe that Bitcoin has the potential to be used in everyday transactions. Proponents of Bitcoin argue that it offers several advantages over traditional payment methods, such as lower transaction fees and greater privacy.

Additionally, Bitcoin's decentralized nature means that it is not subject to the same government regulations and restrictions as traditional payment systems. This has led to some using Bitcoin as a way to circumvent government restrictions on payments or as a way to store wealth in countries with unstable currencies.

While Bitcoin's potential as a payment system is still a subject of debate, it is clear that the development of new technologies and solutions has opened up new possibilities for its use. Whether or not Bitcoin will become a widely used payment method remains to be seen, but its impact on the financial system is sure to be felt for years to come.

Conclusion
The significance of Bitcoin and its impact on the future of money

Bitcoin is a revolutionary technology that has the potential to disrupt the traditional financial system. In this conclusion, we will summarize the key points discussed in this book and reflect on the significance of Bitcoin and its impact on the future of money.

Bitcoin was created in 2008 by an unknown person or group using the pseudonym Satoshi Nakamoto. It is a decentralized digital currency that operates without a central authority or intermediary. Bitcoin is based on a distributed ledger technology called the blockchain, which records every transaction on a decentralized network of nodes.

The decentralized nature of Bitcoin provides several advantages over traditional financial systems. One of the key advantages is that it eliminates the need for intermediaries, such as banks or payment processors, to verify transactions. This not only reduces transaction fees but also allows for faster and more efficient transactions.

Another advantage of Bitcoin is its transparency. Since every transaction is recorded on the blockchain, it is virtually impossible to manipulate the data. This ensures that the integrity of the system is maintained and prevents fraud and corruption.

The use of cryptographic protocols, such as hash functions and digital signatures, ensures the security and authenticity of transactions. The proof-of-work consensus mechanism is used to validate transactions and prevent double-spending.

However, Bitcoin also faces several challenges that need to be addressed for it to achieve mainstream adoption. One of the most pressing challenges is scalability. The current transaction processing capacity of the Bitcoin network is limited, and as more users join the network, the system is becoming increasingly congested.

Another challenge facing Bitcoin is the environmental impact of mining. The process of mining Bitcoin requires a significant amount of energy, which has raised concerns about its sustainability.

The legal and regulatory landscape surrounding Bitcoin is also complex and constantly evolving. Governments around the world are still struggling to define their approach to the regulation of cryptocurrencies, and this uncertainty has hindered the mainstream adoption of Bitcoin.

Despite these challenges, Bitcoin has the potential to revolutionize the financial industry. Its decentralized nature provides greater financial freedom to individuals, and it offers a more secure and transparent way to conduct transactions.

Bitcoin's potential to be used as a store of value has also been recognized by institutional investors, and we have seen a significant increase in the number of companies adding Bitcoin to their balance sheets. This has led to a surge in the price of Bitcoin, and many analysts believe that it will continue to appreciate in value in the coming years.

The potential for Bitcoin to be used in everyday transactions is also growing, with the development of new payment solutions and the increasing acceptance of Bitcoin by merchants and retailers.

In conclusion, Bitcoin is a groundbreaking technology that has the potential to transform the financial industry. Its decentralized nature provides greater financial freedom, and its transparency and security ensure the integrity of the system. However, it also faces several challenges that need to be addressed for it to achieve mainstream adoption. Despite these challenges, the potential impact of Bitcoin on the future of money cannot be ignored, and it will be exciting to see how this technology evolves in the years to come.

The potential for further developments in the Bitcoin system

Bitcoin has come a long way since its inception in 2009, and its development has been remarkable in terms of the number of users, the amount of transactions, and the overall growth of the ecosystem. Despite the challenges faced by the system, it has shown a resilience that suggests it is here to stay. In this chapter, we will explore the potential for further developments in the Bitcoin system, including both technological advancements and social developments.

One of the most significant potential developments for Bitcoin is the implementation of the Lightning Network. The Lightning Network is a second layer solution built on top of the Bitcoin network that allows for instant, high-volume transactions with very low fees. It operates by creating a network of payment channels between users, enabling them to transact without the need to wait for confirmations on the Bitcoin blockchain. The Lightning Network has been in development for several years, and while it is still in its early stages, it has the potential to revolutionize the way Bitcoin is used for everyday transactions.

Another potential development for Bitcoin is the integration of privacy features. While Bitcoin transactions are pseudonymous, meaning that they are not linked to a user's real-world identity, they are still transparent and can be traced back to their origin. This lack of privacy has led to concerns about the potential for surveillance and censorship. There are several proposals for privacy enhancements to the Bitcoin protocol, including the integration of privacy-focused coins like Monero and the implementation of techniques such as zero-knowledge proofs.

Another area of potential development for Bitcoin is in the realm of smart contracts. Smart contracts are self-executing contracts with the terms of the agreement between buyer and seller being directly written into lines of code. While Bitcoin was not designed for smart contracts, there are several projects currently underway to build smart contract functionality on top of the Bitcoin blockchain. One of the most promising of these is Rootstock, a sidechain platform that allows for the execution of smart contracts with Bitcoin as the underlying asset.

Beyond technological advancements, there are also potential developments in the social and regulatory landscape surrounding Bitcoin. One of the most significant of these is the potential for institutional adoption of Bitcoin. While Bitcoin was initially seen as a fringe movement outside of the traditional financial system, its growing popularity and legitimacy have led to increased interest from institutional investors and mainstream financial institutions. If Bitcoin were to become widely adopted by institutional investors, it could lead to a significant increase in demand and a corresponding increase in price.

Regulatory developments are also a significant area of potential development for Bitcoin. While Bitcoin has largely operated outside of the regulatory framework, there are increasing calls for regulation of the cryptocurrency industry. Regulatory clarity could help to reduce uncertainty for businesses operating in the Bitcoin space and increase investor confidence in the ecosystem. However, there is also a risk that overregulation could stifle innovation and growth in the industry.

In conclusion, Bitcoin has come a long way since its inception and has shown a remarkable ability to adapt and evolve in the face of challenges. The potential for further development in the Bitcoin system is significant, both in terms of technological advancements and in the social and regulatory landscape. The future of Bitcoin is uncertain, but it is clear that the system has already had a significant impact on the financial industry and has the potential to continue to do so in the future.

The role of Bitcoin in the wider context of technological innovation and disruption

Bitcoin has gained significant attention and popularity not only as a cryptocurrency but also as a technological innovation that has disrupted the traditional financial system. Its potential impact on the wider context of technological innovation and disruption is worth exploring in this chapter.

Bitcoin is built on a decentralized and distributed technology called blockchain. The blockchain is a public ledger that records all the transactions on the Bitcoin network. The use of blockchain technology has extended beyond Bitcoin and has been adopted by other industries such as supply chain management, healthcare, and real estate. Its ability to provide a transparent and secure way of recording and transferring data has the potential to transform various industries.

Moreover, the development of Bitcoin has given rise to other cryptocurrencies, which have also adopted the blockchain technology. These cryptocurrencies, also known as altcoins, have been designed to address some of the challenges and limitations of Bitcoin. For instance, some altcoins have been created to address the scalability challenges of Bitcoin. These cryptocurrencies have the potential to further disrupt the traditional financial system and provide alternative means of exchange.

Another significant development in the Bitcoin ecosystem is the emergence of decentralized finance (DeFi) platforms. DeFi platforms are built on blockchain technology and provide financial services such as lending, borrowing, and trading without the need for intermediaries such as banks. The use of DeFi platforms has the potential to transform the traditional financial system by providing more access to financial services for people who are excluded from the traditional system.

The development of the Lightning Network is another significant development in the Bitcoin ecosystem. The Lightning Network is a second-layer protocol built on top of the Bitcoin blockchain that allows for faster and cheaper transactions. This development has the potential to address the scalability challenges of Bitcoin and make it a more viable means of exchange.

Moreover, the development of smart contract platforms such as Ethereum has opened up new possibilities for the use of blockchain technology. Smart contracts are self-executing contracts with the terms of the agreement between buyer and seller being directly written into lines of code. The use of smart contracts has the potential to automate various processes and reduce the need for intermediaries.

The emergence of Bitcoin has also led to a shift in the way people view money and its role in society. Bitcoin has been designed to operate independently of any government or central authority. This has given rise to the idea of digital sovereignty, which refers to the idea that individuals should have control over their financial transactions without interference from governments or financial institutions. The potential for greater financial freedom and control is an attractive prospect for many people.

Furthermore, the development of Bitcoin has highlighted the potential for innovation and disruption in other areas of society. The use of decentralized and distributed technologies has the potential to disrupt various industries, from healthcare to education. The use of blockchain technology in supply chain management has the potential to provide greater transparency and accountability in various industries.

In conclusion, the development of Bitcoin has had a significant impact on the wider context of technological innovation and disruption. The use of blockchain technology has extended beyond Bitcoin and has been adopted by other industries. The emergence of altcoins, DeFi platforms, the

Lightning Network, and smart contract platforms has the potential to transform various industries and disrupt the traditional financial system. The development of Bitcoin has also highlighted the potential for innovation and disruption in other areas of society. The potential for greater financial freedom and control has made Bitcoin an attractive prospect for many people. The impact of Bitcoin on the future of technological innovation and disruption is yet to be fully realized, but its potential is immense.

THE END

Key Terms and Definitions

To help you better understand the language and concepts related to aging and older adults, below you will find a list of key terms and their definitions.

1. Bitcoin: A decentralized digital currency that operates on a peer-to-peer network and uses cryptography to secure transactions and control the creation of new units.

2. Blockchain: A decentralized, digital ledger of all Bitcoin transactions that is maintained by a network of computers.

3. Cryptography: The practice of secure communication that makes it difficult for third parties to access, read, or modify data.

4. Digital signature: A digital code that verifies the authenticity of a message, document, or transaction.

5. Decentralization: The distribution of power and control among a network of computers, rather than relying on a central authority or single point of control.

6. Proof-of-work: A consensus mechanism used in the Bitcoin network to confirm transactions and prevent fraudulent activity.

7. Hash function: A mathematical function used to transform data into a fixed-size output, which is used in Bitcoin to secure transactions and prevent tampering.

8. Double-spending: A fraudulent activity where the same Bitcoin is spent more than once, which is prevented in the Bitcoin network through the use of the blockchain and proof-of-work.

9. Scalability: The ability of a system to handle increased traffic and transactions without compromising performance.

10. Store of value: An asset or commodity that maintains its value over time and can be used to store wealth.

11. Mining: The process by which new Bitcoins are created and transactions are verified on the Bitcoin network.

12. Fork: A divergence in the blockchain, which occurs when a group of nodes follow a different set of rules from the rest of the network, leading to the creation of a new blockchain.

13. Wallet: A digital wallet used to store, send, and receive Bitcoins.

14. Digital asset: A digital representation of a real-world asset, such as a stock or currency, which can be traded on a digital platform.

15. Fintech: The use of technology to improve and automate financial services, including banking, insurance, and investment.

Supporting Materials
Bitcoin Whitepaper

According to the original Bitcoin whitepaper (https://bitcoin.org/bitcoin.pdf) that was authored by Satoshi Nakamoto and titled "Bitcoin: A Peer-to-Peer Electronic Cash System.", here are the page numbers that could be covered in each book:

Book 1/3:

Introduction: Pages 1-2

Chapter 1: "Introduction" section on Page 1

Chapter 2: "Transactions" section on Pages 2-4

Chapter 3: "Timestamp Server" section on Pages 4-5

Chapter 4: "Proof-of-Work" section on Pages 5-7

Chapter 5: "Network" section on Pages 7-8

Conclusion: Pages 8-9

Book 2/3:

Introduction: Pages 1-2

Chapter 1: "Introduction" section on Page 1

Chapter 2: "The Economics of Bitcoin" section on Pages 2-3

Chapter 3: "Bitcoin and Financial Inclusion" section on Pages 3-4

Chapter 4: "Bitcoin and Social Implications" section on Pages 4-6

Chapter 5: "Bitcoin and Income Inequality" section on Pages 6-7

Conclusion: Pages 8-9

Book 3/3:

Introduction: Pages 1-2

Chapter 1: "Introduction" section on Page 1

Chapter 2: "Future Directions" section on Pages 2-3

Chapter 3: "Regulatory Landscape" section on Pages 3-4

Chapter 4: "Potential Applications" section on Pages 4-5

Chapter 5: "Bitcoin and the Environment" section on Pages 5-6

Conclusion: Pages 8-9

Potential References

Introduction

Nakamoto, S. (2008). Bitcoin: A Peer-to-Peer Electronic Cash System.

Chapter 1

Overview of the Bitcoin System: Antonopoulos, A. M. (2014). Mastering Bitcoin: Unlocking Digital Cryptocurrencies. O'Reilly Media, Inc.

Chapter 2

Cryptographic Protocols in Bitcoin: Narayanan, A., Bonneau, J., Felten, E., Miller, A., & Goldfeder, S. (2016). Bitcoin and Cryptocurrency Technologies: A Comprehensive Introduction. Princeton University Press.

Chapter 3

Decentralization in Bitcoin: Swan, M. (2015). Blockchain: Blueprint for a New Economy. O'Reilly Media, Inc.

Chapter 4

Technical Details of Bitcoin: Nakamoto, S. (2008). Bitcoin: A Peer-to-Peer Electronic Cash System.

Chapter 5

Limitations and Challenges of Bitcoin: Narayanan, A., Bonneau, J., Felten, E., Miller, A., & Goldfeder, S. (2016). Bitcoin and Cryptocurrency Technologies: A Comprehensive Introduction. Princeton University Press.

Chapter 6

Bitcoin and the Future of Money: Tapscott, D., & Tapscott, A. (2016). Blockchain Revolution: How the Technology Behind Bitcoin Is Changing Money, Business, and the World. Penguin.

Conclusion

Swan, M. (2015). Blockchain: Blueprint for a New Economy. O'Reilly Media, Inc.

www.ingramcontent.com/pod-product-compliance
Lightning Source LLC
LaVergne TN
LVHW021054100526
838202LV00083B/5877